READING POWER

Coming to America

Why Mexican Immigrants Came to America

Lewis K. Parker

The Rosen Publishing Group's
PowerKids Press™
New York

Published in 2003 by The Rosen Publishing Group, Inc.
29 East 21st Street, New York, NY 10010

First Edition

Book Design: Mindy Liu and Erica Clendening

Photo Credits: Cover © AP/Wide World Photos; p. 4 Old Military and Civil Records Branch, National Archives and Records Adminstration; pp. 5, 10 © MapArt; pp. 6–7, 11, 15 © Bettmann/Corbis; p. 7 (inset) © North Wind Picture Archives; pp. 8, 9 © Library of Congress, Prints and Photographs; pp. 12–13 courtesy Chicano Research Collection, Arizona State University Libraries; pp. 16–17 © Chris Rainier/Corbis; pp. 18–19 © Cindy Reiman; p. 20 © Lindsay Hebberd/Corbis; p. 21 © Arthur Schatz/TimePix

Library of Congress Cataloging-in-Publication Data

Parker, Lewis K.
Why Mexican immigrants came to America / Lewis K. Parker.
    p. cm. — (Coming to America)
Summary: Explores Mexican immigration to the United States from before this country existed to the present, and looks at the contributions of Mexican Americans to the culture of the United States.
Includes bibliographical references and index.
ISBN 0-8239-6459-0 (lib. bdg.)
1. Mexican Americans—History—Juvenile literature. 2. Immigrants—United States—History—Juvenile literature. 3. Mexico—Emigration and immigration—History—Juvenile literature. 4. United States—Emigration and immigration—History—Juvenile literature. [1. Mexican Americans—History. 2. Immigrants—History. 3. Mexico—Emigration and immigration. 4. United States—Emigration and immigration.] I. Title.
E184.M5 P37 2003
304.8'73072—dc21

                                        2002000093

Contents

The Mexican-American War

From 1846 to 1848, the United States fought a war against Mexico. It was called the Mexican-American War. The United States won the war.

In 1848, the Treaty of Guadalupe Hidalgo (gwa-duh-LOO-pay hy-DAL-go) stated that Mexico was to give the lands of present-day California, Nevada, Utah, and Texas; most of New Mexico and Arizona; and parts of Colorado and Wyoming to the United States. The United States was to give 15 million dollars to Mexico.

The war ended with a treaty that gave America a large part of Mexico's land. More than 75,000 Mexicans lived on this land. Those Mexicans who chose to stay on the land could also choose to become U.S. citizens.

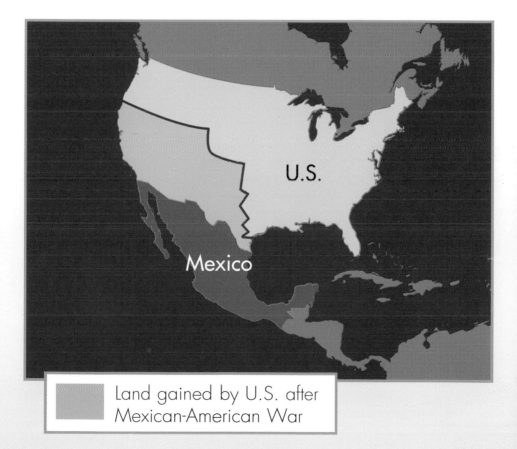

Land gained by U.S. after Mexican-American War

Revolution in Mexico

Porfirio Diaz (POR-fee-ree-oh DEE-az) was the leader of Mexico from 1884 to 1911. He built railroads and started businesses, but he did not treat poor people fairly.

Pancho Villa (above, right) was a leader of the revolution against Porfirio Diaz.

By 1910, Diaz's enemies wanted to get rid of him. They began a revolution to end his rule.

Under the rule of Porfirio Diaz (above) most poor people in Mexico received no education and had to start working when they were very young.

More than one million people were killed in the revolution. Many homes and farms were burned. Many people had no way to earn money.

Thousands of Mexicans escaped across the border into the United States. They wanted to be safe from the troubles in Mexico.

From 1910 to 1930, a small part of Mexico's population left Mexico and went to the United States and other countries.

Mexican people often used cannons in their fight against Diaz's army.

A New Life in the United States

Often, the people of a whole village traveled together across the border. They were looking for jobs and higher pay. However, life in America was not easy for most Mexican immigrants. Much of the work they did was hard and dangerous.

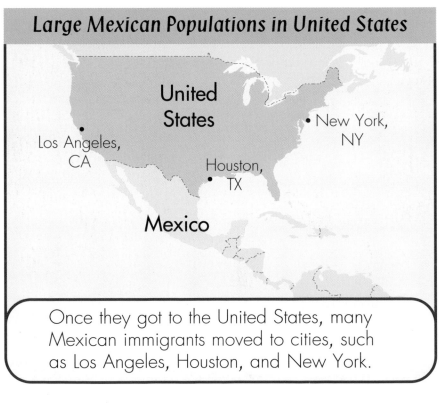

Large Mexican Populations in United States

Once they got to the United States, many Mexican immigrants moved to cities, such as Los Angeles, Houston, and New York.

Most Mexican immigrants found jobs working on railroads, in mines, or on farms.

Back to Mexico

During the Great Depression of the 1930s, jobs were hard to find in the United States. Many people in the United States believed that Mexican immigrants were taking jobs away from Americans. The U.S. government started to send Mexican immigrants back to Mexico.

These Mexican immigrants in Arizona are waiting for a train that will take them back to Mexico.

The Fact Box

By 1930, most of the Mexican immigrants who were still in the United States lived in California or Texas.

During World War II, the U.S. government needed people to work on farms and to build railroads. The United States and Mexico set up a program that allowed Mexicans to work in the United States for a short period of time. Soon, the laws were changed so that more Mexicans could stay for a longer time.

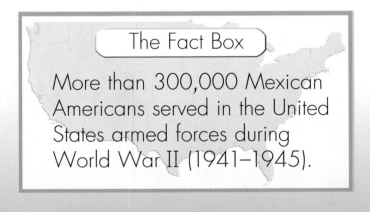

The Fact Box

More than 300,000 Mexican Americans served in the United States armed forces during World War II (1941–1945).

About five million Mexicans worked in the United States as part of the *bracero* program. *Bracero* comes from *brazo*, which means "strong arm" in the Spanish language.

Many Mexicans still come to America, seeking a better way of life. Today, the U.S. government allows only a small number of immigrants into the country each year.

In 1924, the Border Patrol was created to stop people from illegally entering the United States.

More than three million Mexicans live illegally in the United States today. Illegally crossing the border is a very dangerous journey. Many Mexicans die before safely reaching the United States.

"We had to go through the hills and the desert, and we had to swim through a river. I was a little scared. Then we came to a highway and a man was there with a van. Our guide said hello to the man, and the man jumped into the car and we ran and jumped in, too. He began to drive down the highway fast, and we knew that we were safe, in the United States."

— An illegal Mexican immigrant

Many Mexican immigrants face great dangers to come to America to find a better way of life.

Mexican Americans Today

Today, over 20 million people in the United States can trace their roots to Mexico. Mexican immigrants have played an important part in the growth of the United States.

This is the start of a Mexican-American rodeo in Texas. Mexican Americans are proud of their past and the part they played in the growth of America.

Cesar Chavez was a Mexican American who fought for the rights of farmworkers. He was a hero to many people because he made the lives of thousands of these workers better.

Glossary

bracero (bra-**sehr**-oh) the Spanish word for worker or hired hand

citizen (**siht**-uh-zuhn) a native of a country who has the right to live there

dangerous (**dayn**-juhr-uhs) likely to cause danger or harm

education (ehj-uh-**kay**-shuhn) the system of teaching and learning; the knowledge that results from schooling

Great Depression (**grayt** dih-**prehsh**-uhn) the period (1929—1939) during which many people lost their jobs, and many banks and businesses closed

illegally (**ih**-lee-guh-lee) when someone does something that is against the law

immigrant (**ihm**-ih-gruhnt) a person who comes into a country to live there

revolution (rehv-uh-**loo**-shuhn) a period of change from one type of government to another, usually caused by fighting

treaty (**tree**-tee) an understanding, signed and agreed upon by each nation

Resources

Books

North Across the Border:
The Story of the Mexican Americans
by Lila Perl
Benchmark Books (2001)

The Mexican American Family Album
by Dorothy and Thomas Hoobler
Oxford University Press Children's Books (1998)

Web Sites

Due to the changing nature of Internet links, PowerKids
Press has developed an online list of Web sites related
to the subjects of this book. This site is updated regularly.
Please use this link to access the list:

http://www.powerkidslinks.com/cta/mex/

Index

Word Count: 417

Note to Librarians, Teachers, and Parents

If reading is a challenge, Reading Power is a solution! Reading Power is perfect for readers who want high-interest subject matter at an accessible reading level. These fact-filled, photo-illustrated books are designed for readers who want straightforward vocabulary, engaging topics, and a manageable reading experience. With clear picture/text correspondence, leveled Reading Power books put the reader in charge. Now readers have the power to get the information they want and the skills they need in a user-friendly format.